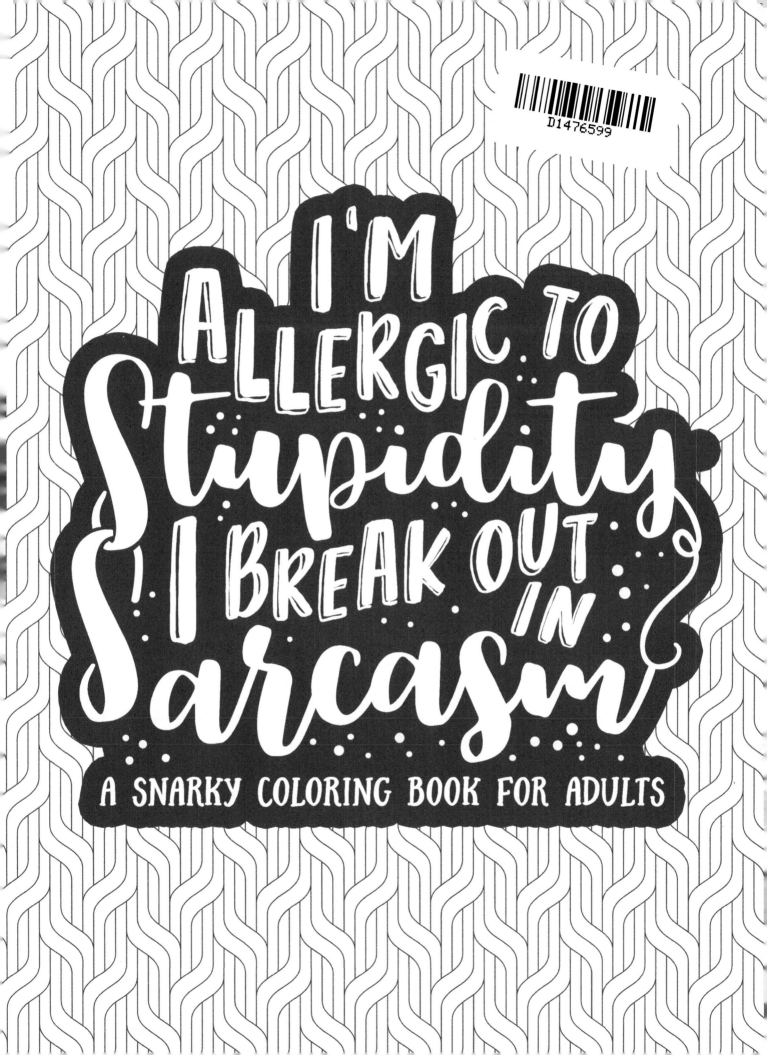

I'M ALLERGIC TO Stupidity I BREAK OUT IN Sarcasm

A SNARKY COLORING BOOK FOR ADULTS

Want free goodies?
Email us at freebies@pbleu.com

@papeteriebleu

Papeterie Bleu

Shop our other books at
www.pbleu.com

Wholesale distribution through Ingram Content Group
www.ingramcontent.com/publishers/distribution/wholesale

For questions and customer service, email us at
support@pbleu.com

FREE PDF DOWNLOAD
OF THIS BOOK

www.pbleu.com/snarkyAF4

YOUR DOWNLOAD CODE: SNK484

 @papeteriebleu

 Papeterie Bleu

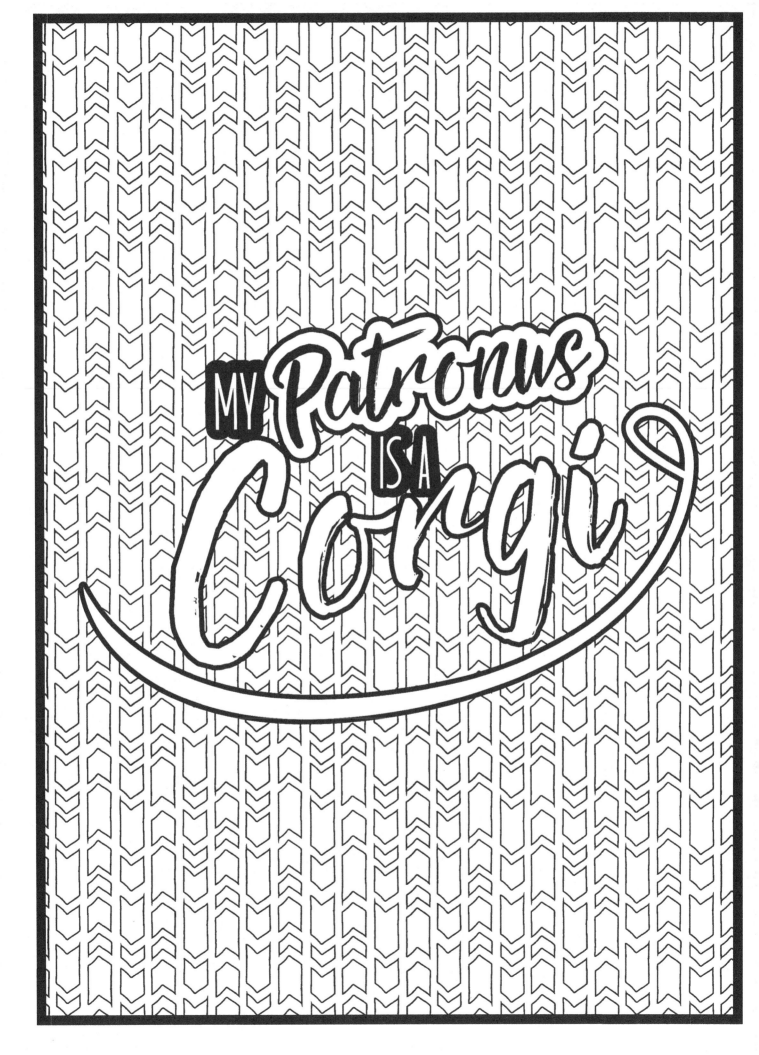

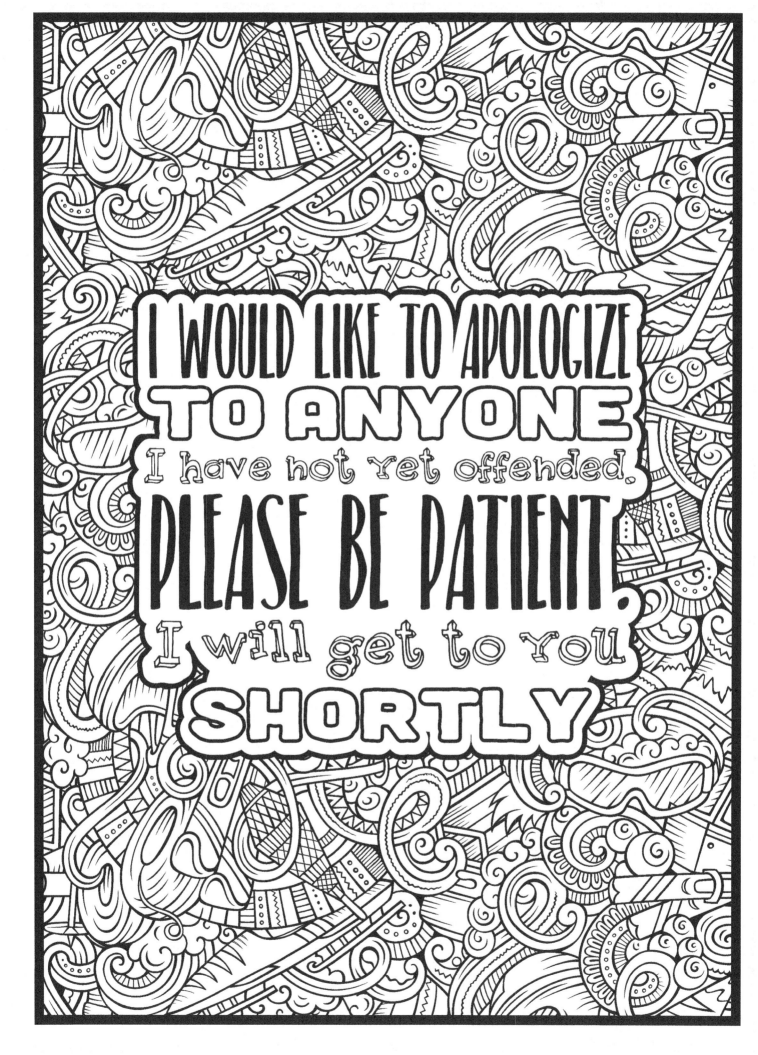

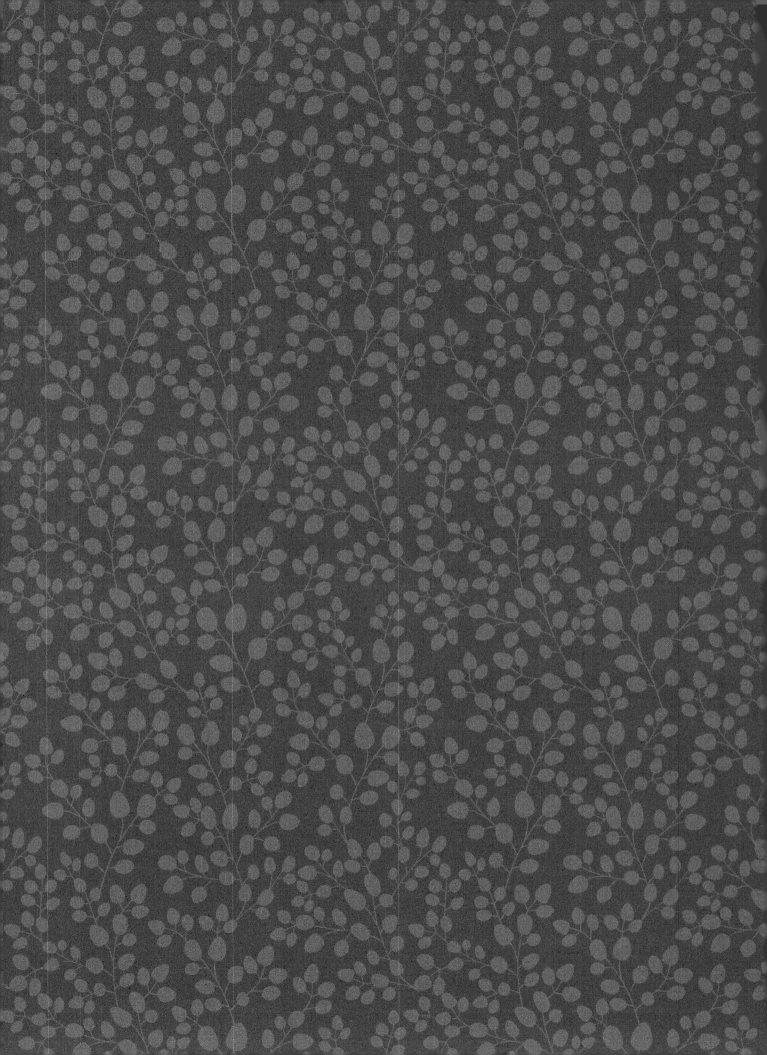

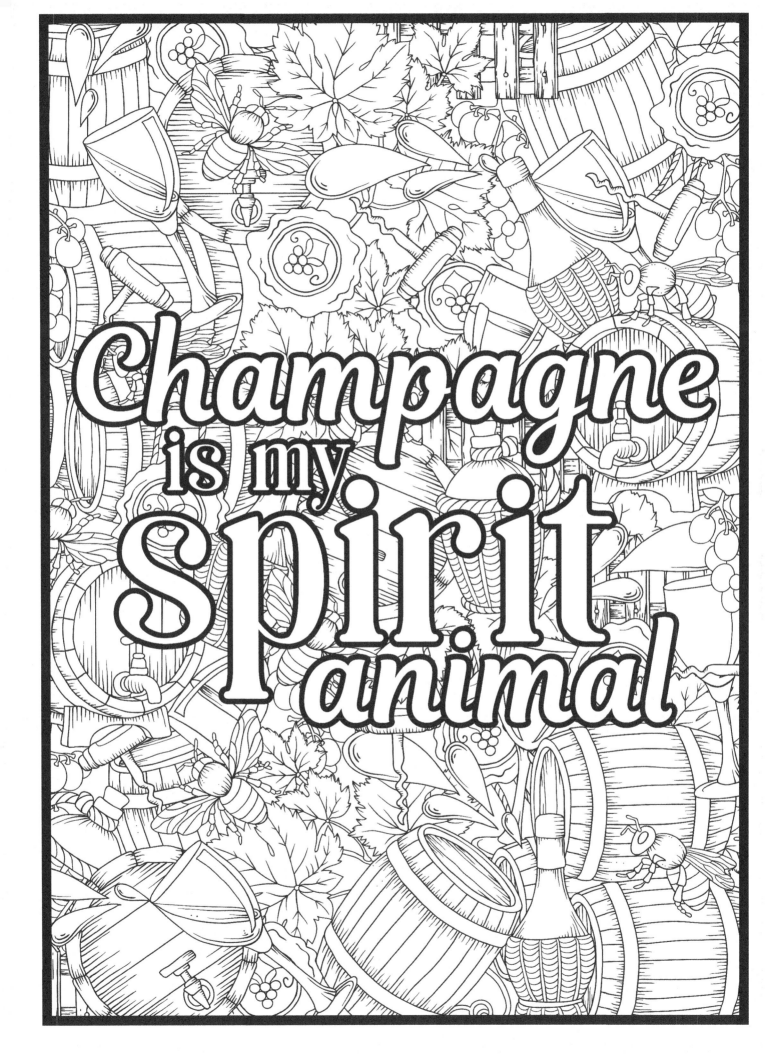

You have a right to your opinions I just don't want to hear them

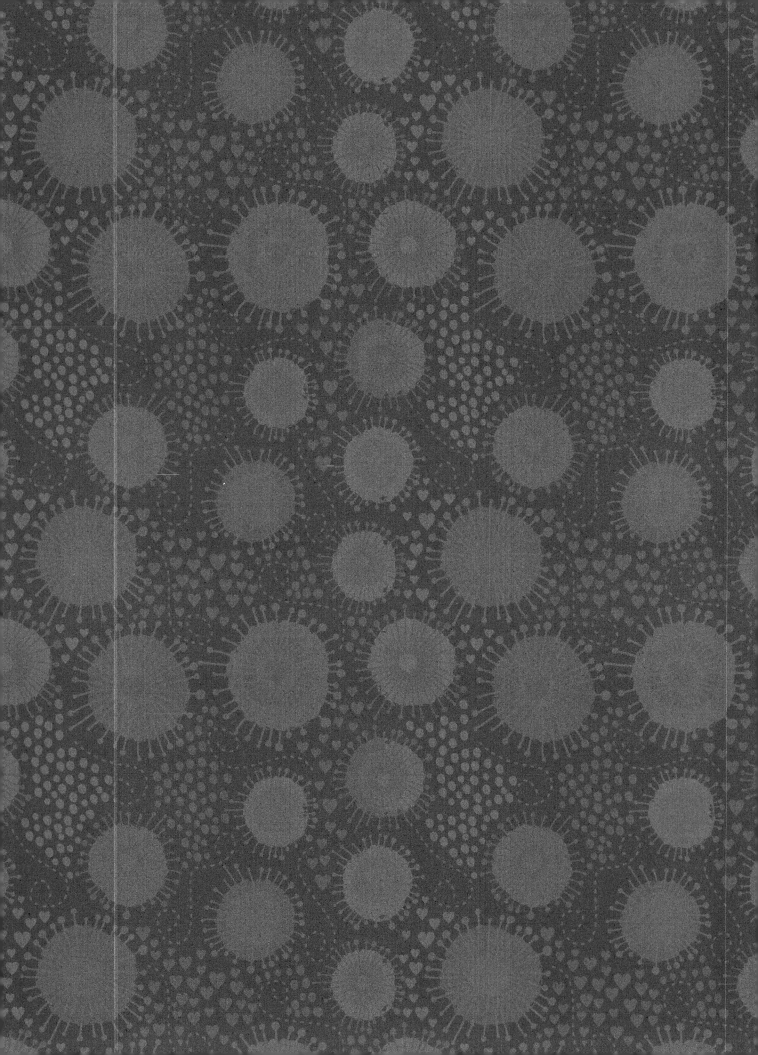

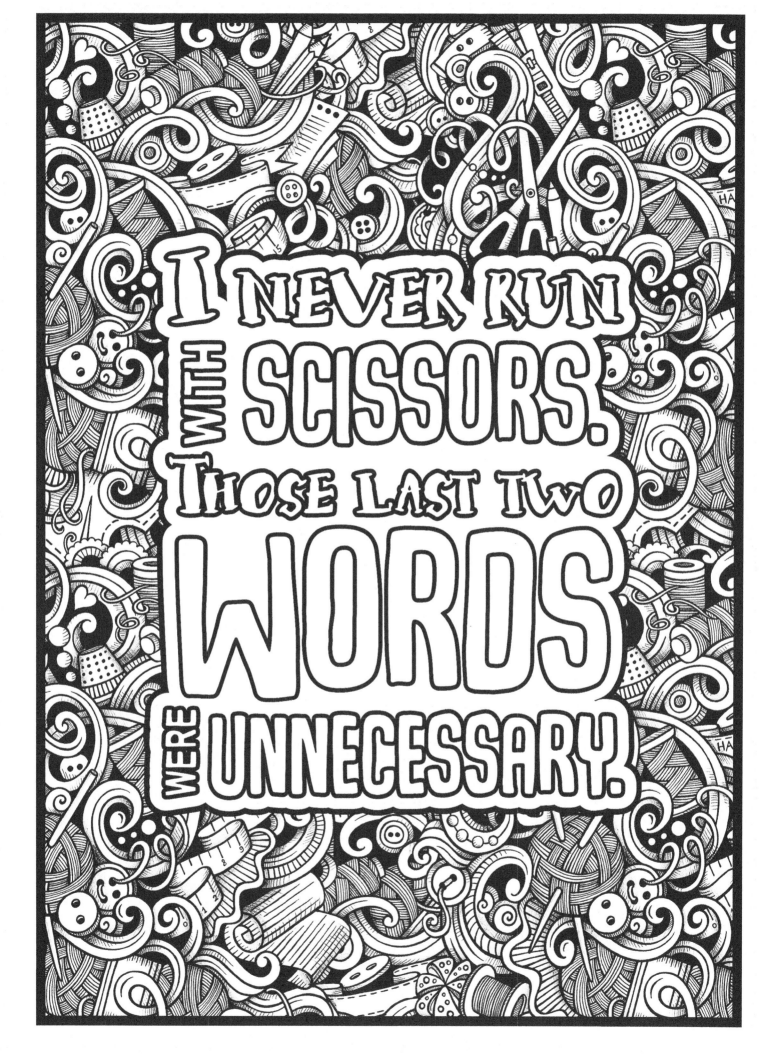

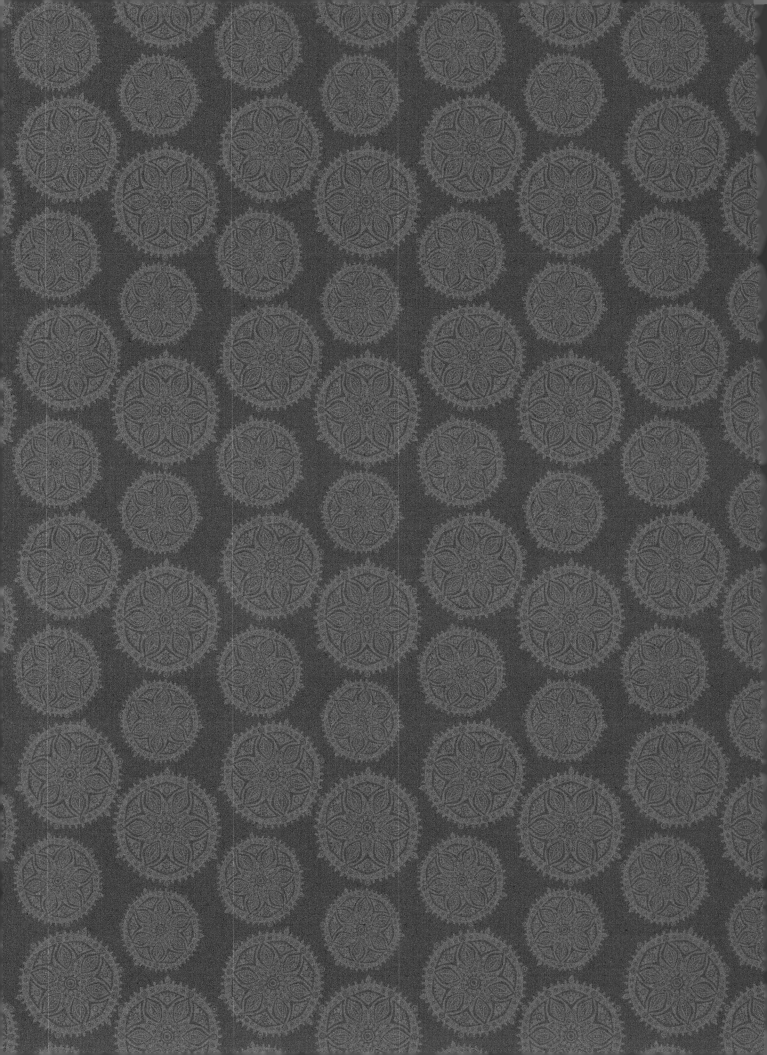

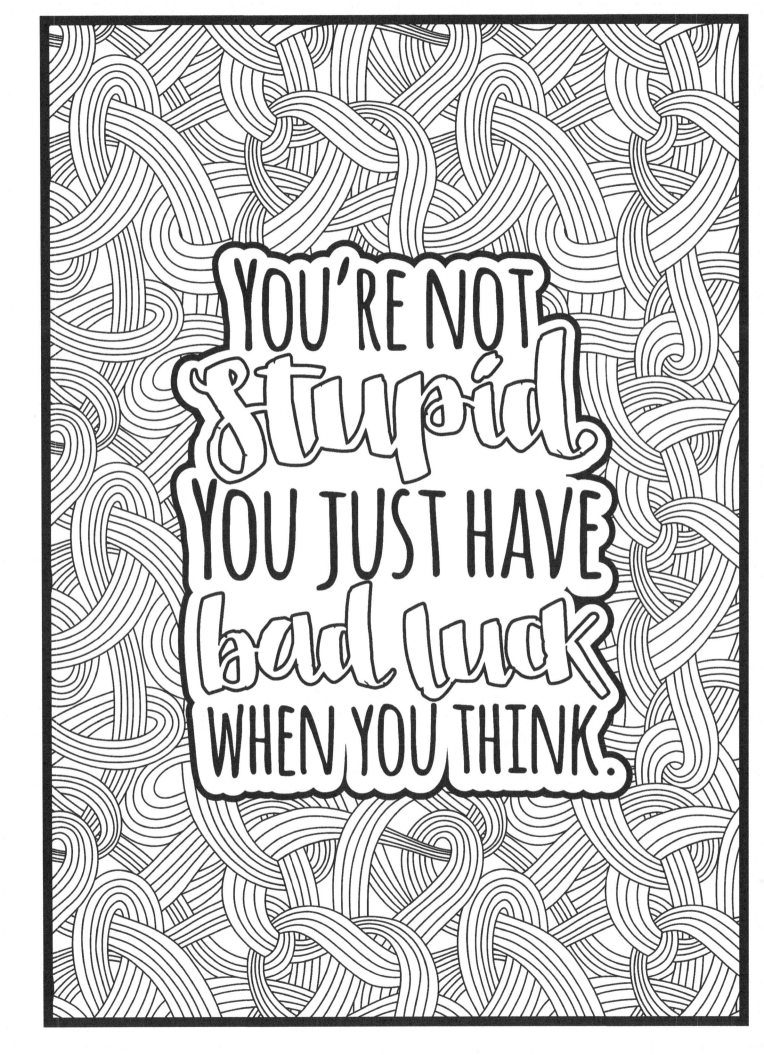

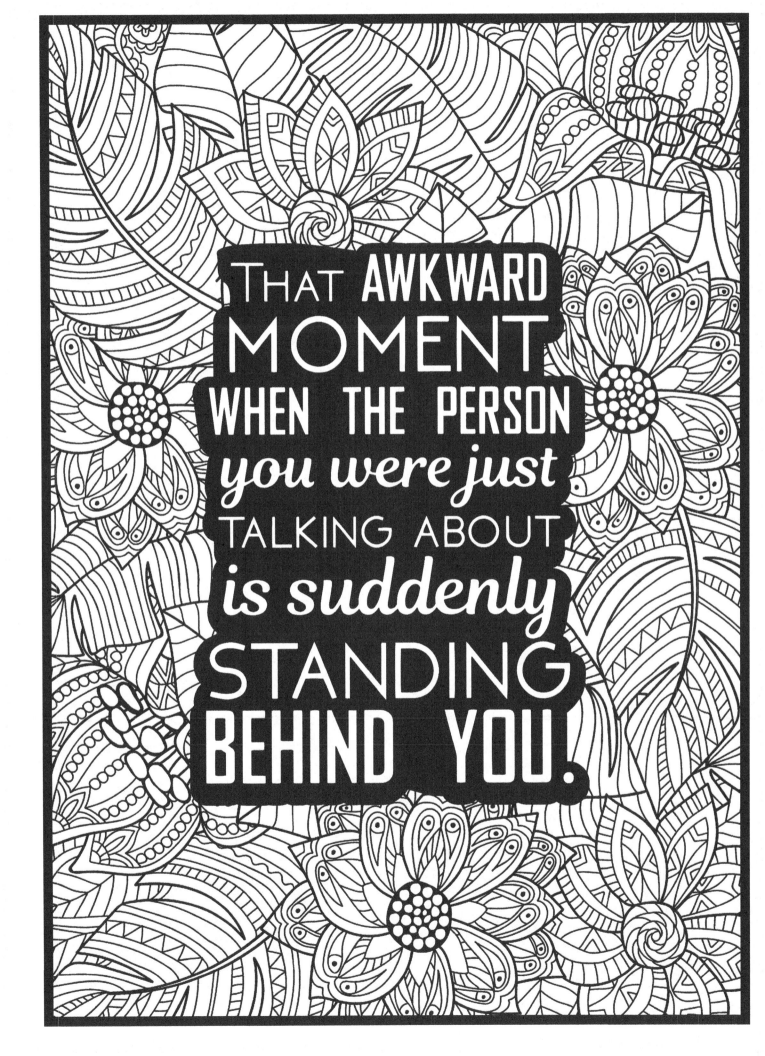

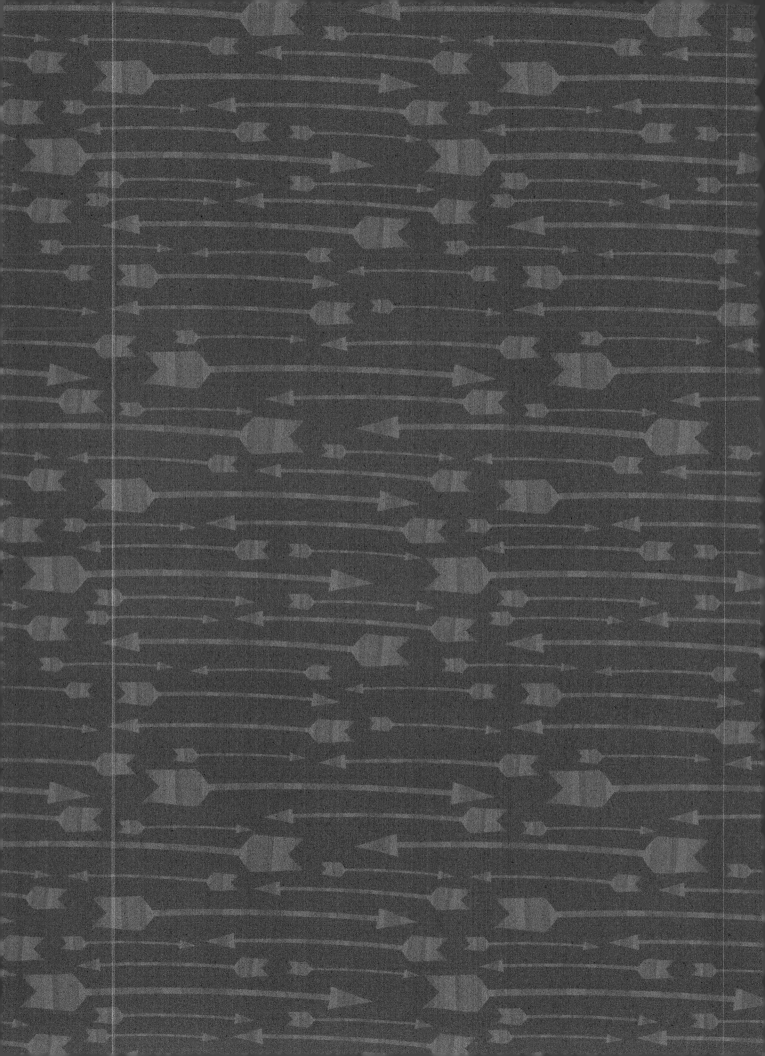

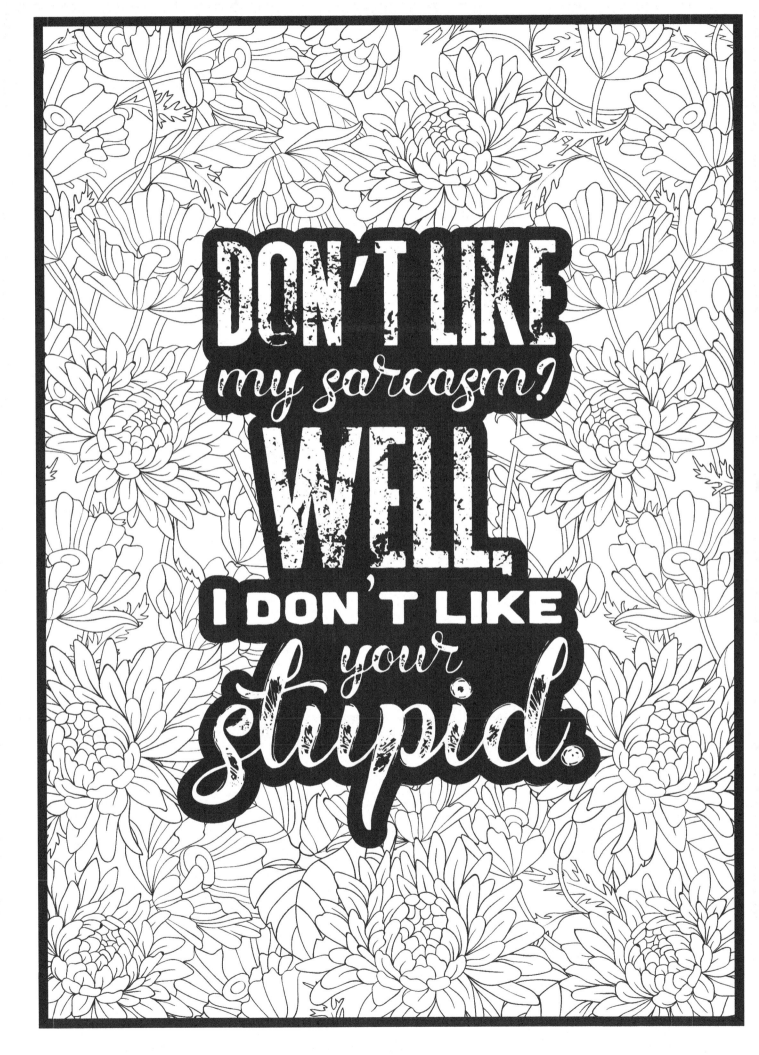

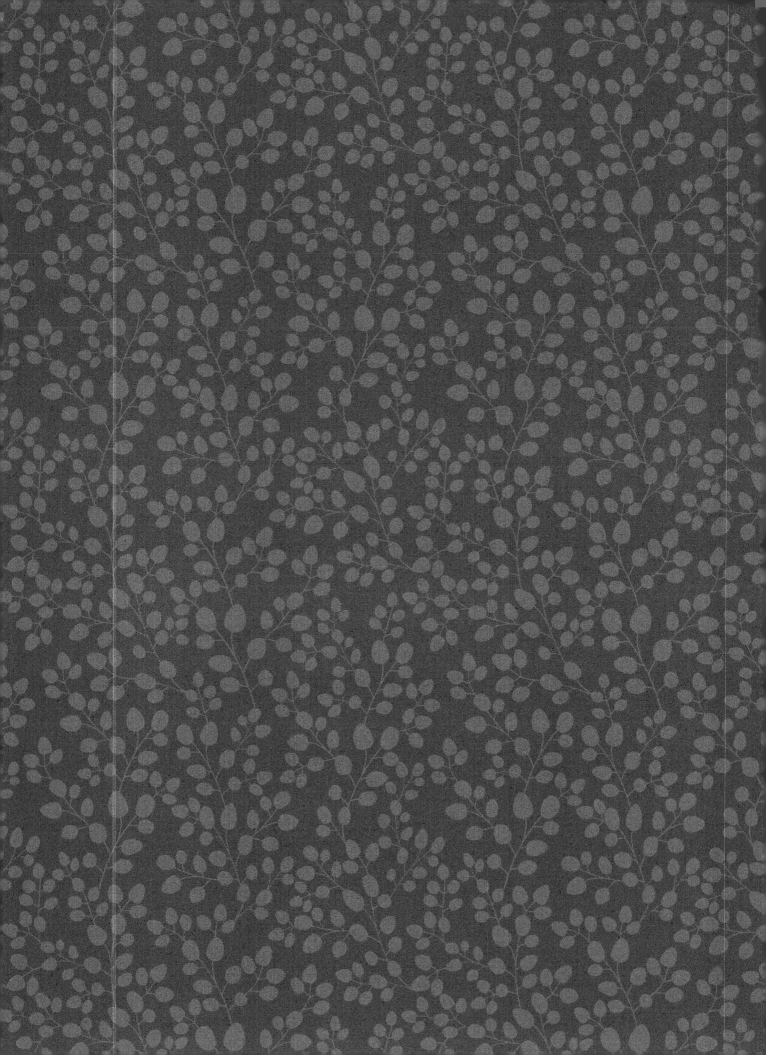

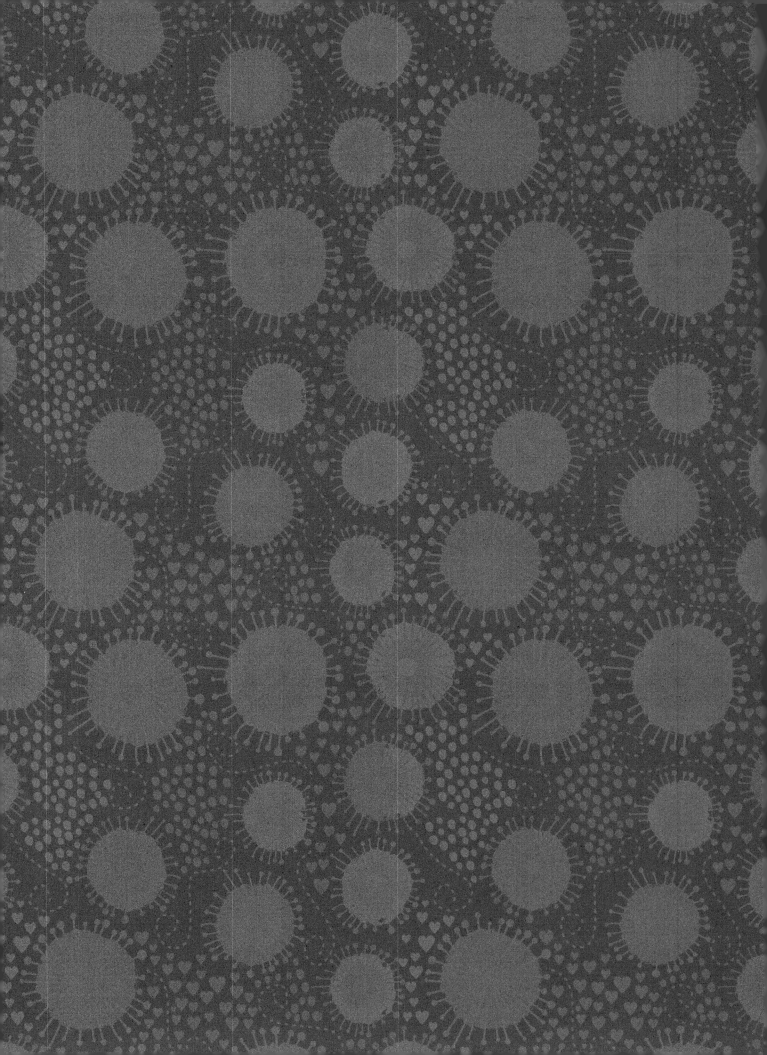

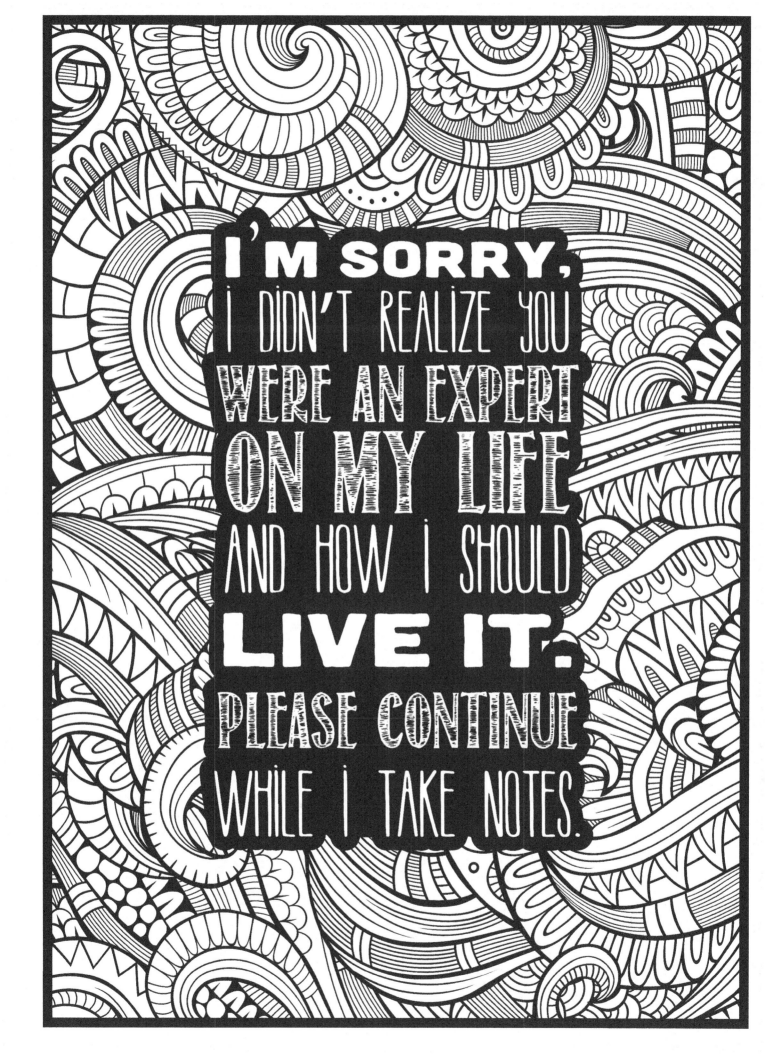

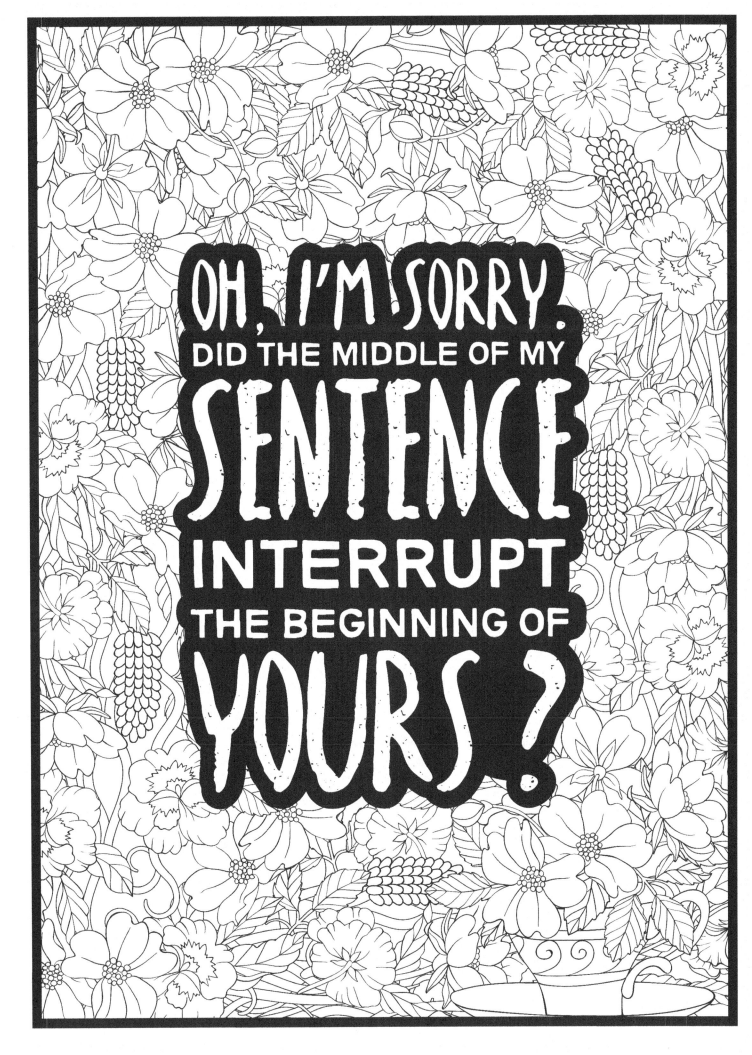

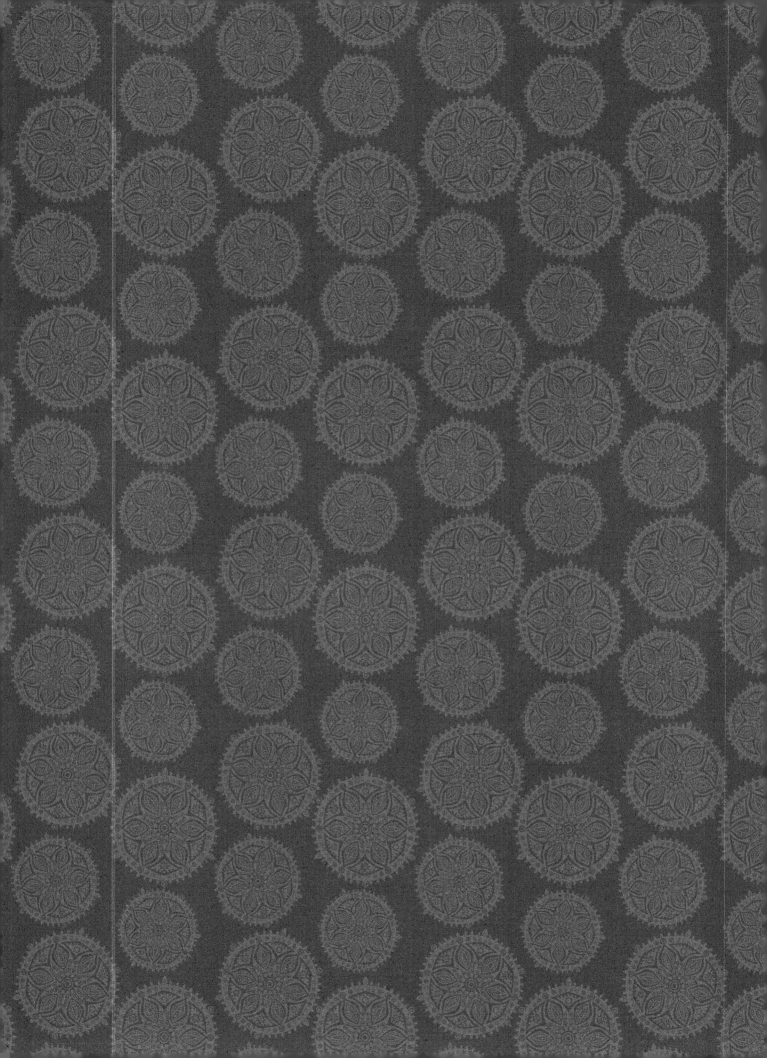

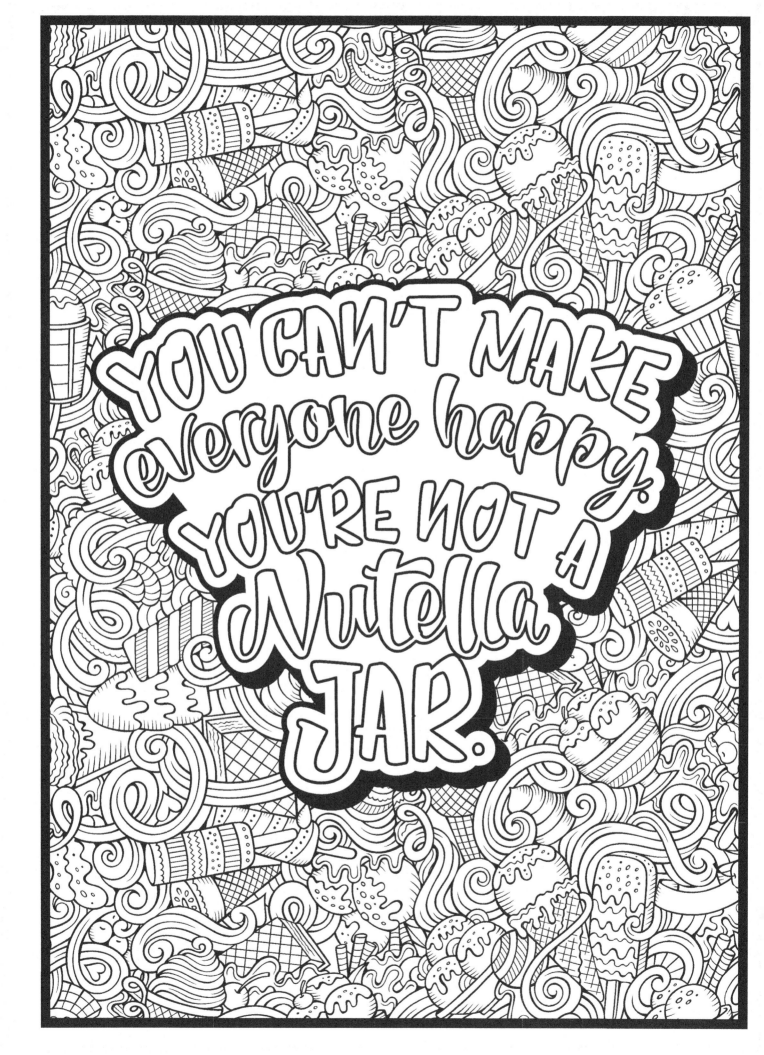

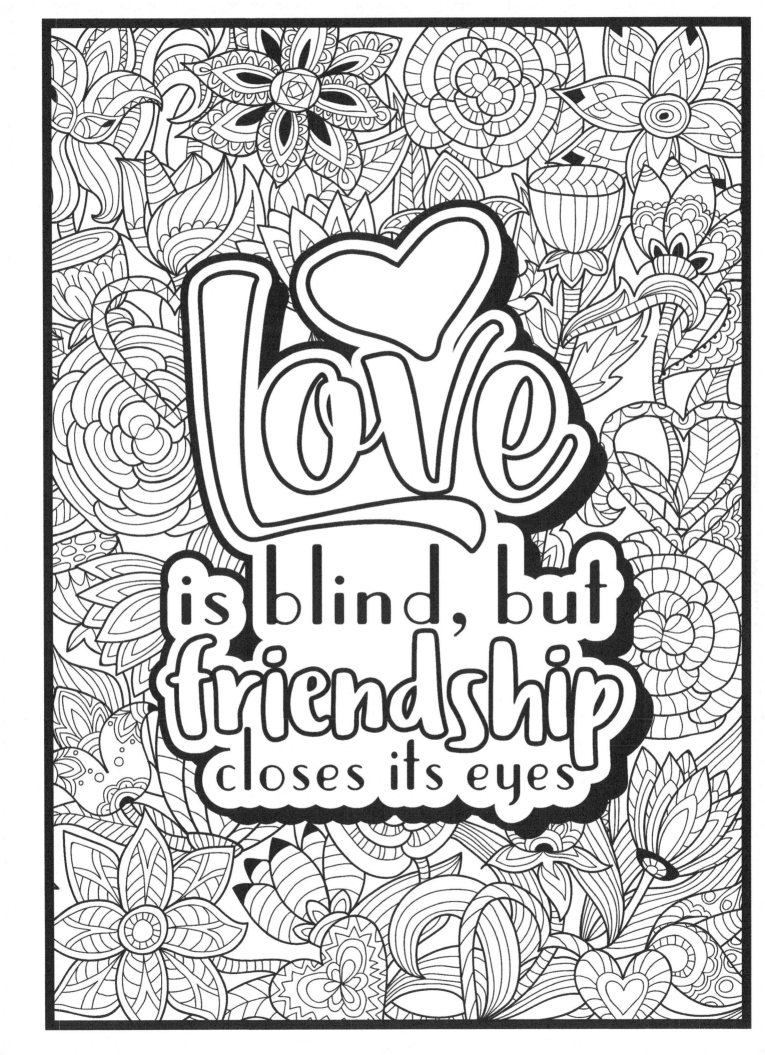

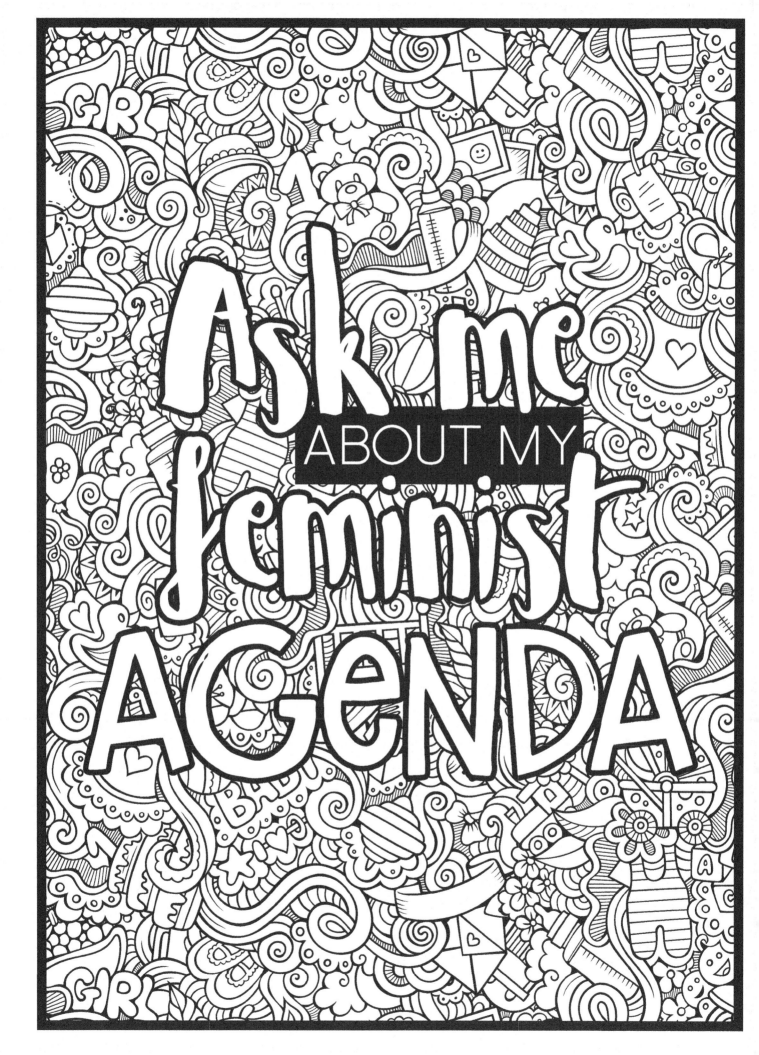

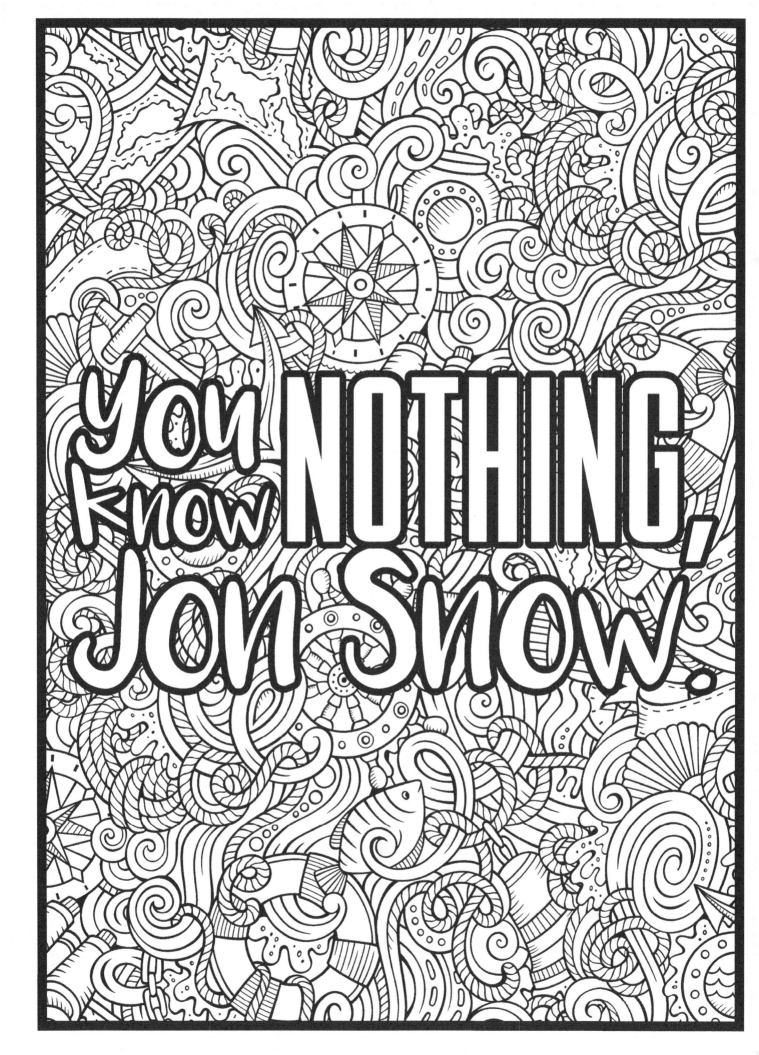

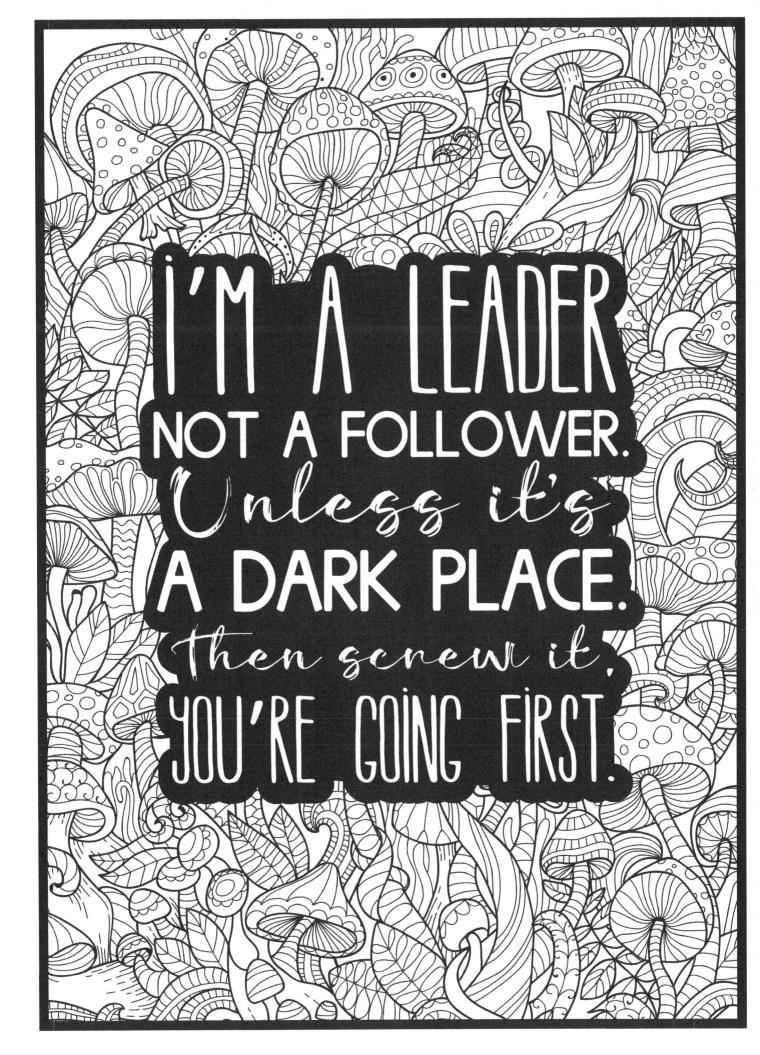

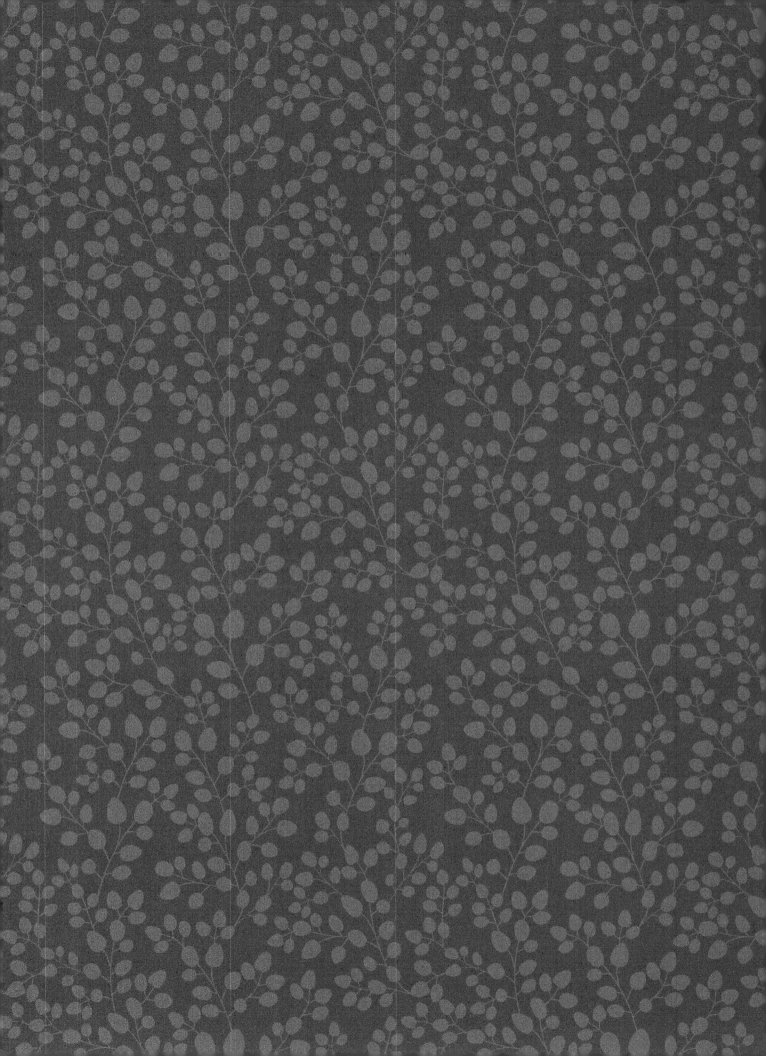

FREE PDF DOWNLOAD
OF THIS BOOK

www.pbleu.com/snarkyAF4

YOUR DOWNLOAD CODE: SNK484

 @papeteriebleu

 Papeterie Bleu

Want free goodies?
Email us at freebies@pbleu.com

@papeteriebleu

Papeterie Bleu

Shop our other books at
www.pbleu.com

Wholesale distribution through Ingram Content Group
www.ingramcontent.com/publishers/distribution/wholesale

For questions and customer service, email us at
support@pbleu.com

Made in the USA
Coppell, TX
31 May 2020